DISNEY'S DINOSAUR

Joke Book

JUSTINE AND RO

BEHIND-THE-SCENE
PROVIDED BY SER

PUFFIN BOOKS

PUFFIN BOOKS

Published by the Penguin Group
Penguin Books Ltd, 27 Wrights Lane, London W8 5TZ, England
Penguin Putnam Inc., 375 Hudson Street, New York, New York 10014, USA
Penguin Books Australia Ltd, Ringwood, Victoria, Australia
Penguin Books Canada Ltd, 10 Alcorn Avenue, Toronto, Ontario, Canada M4V 3B2
Penguin Books (NZ) Ltd, Private Bag 102902, NSMC, Auckland, New Zealand

On the World Wide Web at: www.penguin.com

Penguin Books Ltd, Registered Offices: Harmondsworth, Middlesex, England

First published in the USA by Disney Press 2000
Published in Great Britain by Puffin Books 2000
1

Made and printed in England by Clays Ltd, St Ives plc

British Library Cataloguing in Publication Data
A CIP catalogue record for this book is available from the British Library

ISBN 0–141–30962–8

LAUGHING WITH LEMURS

Why doesn't Plio's daughter feel like laughing today?

Because she's sometimes Suri-us.

What smells most on Lemur Island?

Your nose.

When Zini was feeling grumpy, what did he tell Aladar to do?

'Just lemur alone.'

Suri: What's the best thing to put into fresh fruit?

Zini: Your teeth.

Why was Zini practising his handwriting before the lemur dating ceremony?

He wanted to be the most legible bachelor in the tribe.

**Why did Zini dance
with a raisin?**

He couldn't get a date.

**Why did Aladar's
egg wind up on
Lemur Island?**

It beat being scrambled!

**Why was Aladar so
surprised when the
lemur troupe threw him
a surprise birthday party?**

Because it wasn't his birthday.

**Where did Aladar's
egg fall when it was
dropped by the
pteranodon?**

Down.

An egg was found up in a tree,
By lemurs Yar, Plio, and Zini.
Cried Yar: 'It's a monster!'
Plio said, 'You're wrong, Dad.
Looks like a baby to me!'

Zını: I'm glad they named me Zını.

Aladar: Why?

Zını: Because that's what everybody calls me.

Zını: I'm a pretty good comedıan.

Aladar: Don't make me laugh.

Why dıdn't Aladar speak to Zını for three whole hours?

He didn't want to interrupt.

Surı: How do baby pteranodons learn to fly?

Zini: They wing it!

Suri: How many lemurs can one carnotaur eat on an empty stomach?

Zini: One. After that, his stomach wouldn't be empty.

Why did Zini feel as if he owed money after the dating ceremony?

Because he was left a-lone.

Zini: What holds up the moon?

Suri: The moonbeams!

WEATHER YOU'RE READY OR NOT!

What did Aladar change when the meteorites fell in his path?

His direction.

What time is it when a meteor shower hits?

Time to panic!

Where is a good place to be during a meteor shower?

Anywhere but there!

Suri: What do you call a bigger meteor hole?

Zini: A greater crater!

What did the dust say to the rain?

'Stop! Or my name will be mud.'

Suri: Is it better to cross the sea on a full stomach or an empty stomach?

Zini: It's better to cross the sea on a swimming dinosaur.

Plio: Were you relieved when we finally made it to the mainland?

Aladar: I shore was.

Aladar: Did you hear the joke about the sea?

Zini: Never mind. It's too deep for me.

Aladar: What's the difference between the land and the sea?

Zini: The land is dirt-y and the sea is tide-y.

Suri: What do you get when you toss a dinosaur into a rolling sea?

Zini: Wet.

HAVE YOU HERD THESE?

What happened to the lost iguanodon?

Nobody's herd!

Suri: What did Aladar say when he first saw dinosaurs like him in the Herd?

Zini: Iguana be pals?

Why can't you surprise iguanodons?

Because they've herd it all.

Why do the iguanodons want to change their name?

Herd to say.

Baylene: Why was the lost Herd in the last place we looked for them?

Eema: Because then we stopped looking!

The Herd was quite
a rough bunch.

They'd stomp and push
and crunch.

Aladar joined in
And the lemurs with him –

It beat being a raptor
pack's lunch!

MIGRATION MADNESS

**What is the hardest thing
for a stampeding brachiosaur
to catch?**

Its breath.

**What's worse than having
a hungry carnotaur chasing
you?**

Having two hungry carnotaurs
chasing you!

If the dinosaurs are doomed to a dry, dusty, disagreeable march through the desert, how many 'd's are there in all?

None. There's only an 'a' and two 'l's.

Neera: What do you do when you see Baylene coming?

Aladar: Hope she sees you!

When ten carnotaurs were chasing Aladar, what time was it?

Ten after one!

Aladar: What did Bruton pick up during the migration?

Eema: The pace!

Aladar: During the migration, what did Baylene and Eema want to keep?

Suri: Up!

Suri: How tall are most carnotaurs?

Zini: I don't know, but they're always above two feet.

Neera: How many are ten ailing dinosaurs plus ten more ailing dinosaurs?

Aladar: Twenty sicks.

Suri: Why was Kron like your left foot when he said, 'Only the strong deserve to survive'?

Zini: Because he was not right!

Suri: What do raptors wait for?

Zini: Their chance!

DRY-LAKE LUNACY

Suri: How can you still get wet at a dry lake?

Plio: It dampens your spirits.

Plio: Where can you sink if there's no water?

Aladar: Into despair.

Suri: How did Aladar invent the first well?

Zini: He told Baylene to move her feet in the mud and said, 'Well, dig!'

Crossing a desert most dreary
Was making Eema feel weary.
Then Baylene dug a well,
The water was swell,
And Eema was suddenly cheery.

Neera: You like kids, I see.

Aladar: Well, the skinny ones can be a little chewy.

Aladar: So you don't think Yar would make a good guide?

Eema: Yar couldn't find his shadow on a sunny day!

Suri: What did the orphans learn when Aladar showed them how to get water?

Zini: To dig teamwork.

Plio: Are you still digging for water?

Baylene: No. I'm tired of the hole business.

Plio: During the migration, what was Aladar hoping to keep Neera from falling into?

Yar: The distance.

The dinosaur herd was in need.
They rushed at the lake —
a stampede!
But working together,
Like birds of a feather,
They found was much
better than greed.

CAVE CRAZIES

Aladar: Why was the cave like a stomach pain?

Baylene: It was cramped.

Yar: When is a cave no longer a cave?

Zini: When there's been a cave-in!

Eema: Do you mind being stuck in this cave?

Baylene: Well, I have no room to complain.

Why did Eema think the cave floor was bumpy?

She was sitting on Url!

Yar: If you could change one thing about carnotaurs what would it be?

Suri: Their direction! They're headed this way!

Plio: We can't just leave Bruton here.

Eema: We can if we move fast enough!

Baylene: What can you put in a wall that makes it smaller?

Eema: A hole.

Baylene: When does a brake mean go, not stop?

Eema: When it's a brake-through.

Url is quite bumpy — not dainty.
Some might think his looks quaint.
Covered with plates
Harder than slates,
Sturdy little thing, ain't he?

EGGS-A-LENT DINOSAURS

Baylene: Why is a nest of eggs called a clutch?

Eema: Well, you wouldn't want to drop them!

How do dinosaur parents encourage their babies?

They egg them on!

What do you get from mixed-up dinosaur parents?

Scrambled eggs.

Did you hear the joke about the dinosaur egg?

It cracked me up in a big way!

Do you know how long iguanodon eggs need to hatch?

The same as short iguanodon eggs.

Why did Aladar suddenly feel cold surrounded by grateful dinosaurs at the Nesting Grounds?

The place was full of fans!

What size are iguanodon eggs?

Eggs-tra large.

GAMES WITH NAMES

Suri: What does a carnotaur call a running microceratops?

Zini: Fast food.

What's the dizziest dinosaur?

Tricera-tops.

Suri: Do you know how to spell Aladar backwards?

Zini: A-L-A-D-A-R-B-A-C-K-W-A-R-D-S.

Which dinosaur used to hunt for synonyms?

Thesaurus.

What dinosaur can't stay out in the rain?

Stegosaur-rust!

Which dinosaur never gave up, no matter how many times he failed?

The try-try-again-atops.

Neera: What's even better than a microcera?

Aladar: A microceratops.

What happens when a pteranodon flies for a long time?

He gets ptired.

What do you call a plated dinosaur when he is asleep?

A stego-snorus.

What do you call an iguanodon that talks and talks and talks?

A dinobore!

Dinosaurs who ate other dinosaurs were called carnivores. What were the dinosaurs they ate called?

Dinner-saurs.

Why was it hard for Url to jump?

Because his ankylo-sore.

Why did Kron kick the duck-billed hadrosaur out of the Herd?

He had a fowl mouth.

Suri: Why is Baylene so grumpy today?

Zini: Well, she is a sore-opod.

WACKIEST DINOSAUR JOKES EVER!

Can a microceratops jump higher than a tree?

Yes, a tree can't jump at all!

Why doesn't a microceratops jump when it's sad?

Because it's too unhoppy.

Suri: Why does Baylene have such a long neck?

Zini: Because her head is so far from her body.

Zini: What has a long neck, four legs, a long tail, and purple spots?

Suri: I don't know, what?

Zini: A brachiosaur.

Suri: But brachiosaurs don't have purple spots!

Zini: I know. I added those to make it harder.

Why are tall dinosaurs the laziest?

Because they lie longer on the ground.

Suri: How do you spell dinosaur?

Zini: D-I-N-O-S-A-U . . .

Suri: Go on, what's at the end of it?

Zini: Its tail!

Zini: When do iguanodons have four eyes?

Suri: When there are two of them!

Suri: Why did the carnotaur cross the road?

Zini: Because the chicken hadn't evolved yet.

Why did the other carnotaur cross the road?

To prove he wasn't chicken.

Neera: What do you get for the biggest creature who ever walked the planet?

Aladar: Out of the way!

What did one insectivore say to another?

'Time sure is fun when you're having flies!'

Suri: How do you make a statue of an iguanodon?

Zini: Get a big stone and cut away everything that doesn't look like an iguanodon.

Baylene: Oh, my neck is so sore. I'm going to ask Plio for one of her healing flowers.

Zini: Neck's weak?

Baylene: No, I'm going to ask her right now.

Why did raptors eat raw meat?

They didn't know how to cook.

Yar: I see you and Aladar are building a new nest.

Neera: Yes, that's the only kind we build.

Suri: Lightning scares me.

Plio: Don't worry. It will be over in a flash.

Why did Suri ride Aladar through the desert?

He was too heavy to carry.

Raptors have sharp,
slashing claws

Matched up with
shiny-toothed maws.

If you see 'em coming,
Just start running,

To avoid getting snapped
in their jaws!

How much fur can you get from a carnotaur?

As fur as you can get!

Zini: Last night, I couldn't get to sleep so I started counting dinosaurs. I got up to 25,000.

Suri: Then you fell asleep?

Zini: No, by then it was time to get up!

Aladar: Did you hear the joke about the brachiosaur?

Zini: Don't tell me. It's way over my head.

Aladar: How many leaves grow on that tree?

Suri: All of them.

Why did the hungry dinosaur suddenly stop running?

He needed brake-fast!

When can Baylene hide under a single leaf and not get wet?

When it's not raining.

What kind of dinosaurs live in the desert?

Thirsty ones.

Where was Aladar when the sun went down?

In the dark!

Where was Aladar when the meteors came down?

In trouble!

Plio: Do you like using Aladar's tail as a slide?

Suri: It has its ups and downs.

Suri: Why are dinosaurs huge and scaly?

Zini: Because if they were small and furry, they'd be lemurs!

Plio: After that long trip through the desert, you look pretty dirty, Zini.

Zini: If you think I look pretty dirty, you should see how much prettier I am when I'm clean!

Aladar: Can you name ten dinosaurs in ten seconds?

Zini: Sure. Eight iguanodons and two brachiosaurs.

What's a pteranodon's favourite drink?

Saur milk.

What did Suri say when she slid down Baylene's neck?

'So long.'

**Why was the iguanodon
afraid of the carnotaur?**

He was clawstrophobic!

**Suri: I don't know how to
communicate with these huge
dinosaurs. How do you talk to
a brachiosaur?**

Zini: Just use really big words.

**Suri: Why did Url think the
whole Herd was learning maths?**

Zini: Because Aladar said, 'Everyone
counts.'

If carnotaurs invite you for lunch,
I have a guess and a hunch:
You'd better not go.
If you don't say no,
It might be you that they munch!

KNOCK-KNOCKASAURUS!

KnOcK, kNoCk.

Who's there?

YAR.

Yar who?

**YAR-WHOOO!
ARE WE HAVING FUN YET?**

KnOcK, kNoCk.

Who's there?

TURNER.

Turner who?

**TURNER ROUND, THERE'S
A CARNOTAUR BREATHING
DOWN YOUR NECK!**

KnOcK, kNoCk.

Who's there?

AH-CHOO!

Ah-choo who?

AH CHEW YOU UP! ROAR!

KnOcK, kNoCk.

Who's there?

CLIFF CUMMING.

Cliff Cumming who?

CLIFF COMING, BETTER JUMP!

KnOcK, kNoCk.

Who's there?

HUGO.

Hugo who?

**HUGO ON AHEAD.
I'M TOO TIRED TO MOVE.**

KnOcK, kNoCk.

Who's there?

LEMUR.

Lemur who?

**LEMUR ALONE,
CAN'T YOU SEE I'M BUSY?**

KnOcK, kNoCk.

Who's there?

URL.

Url who?

**URL SHOW YOU WHO'S
A TOUGH DINOSAUR!**

KnOcK, kNoCk.

Who's there?

ORPHAN.

Orphan who?

**ORPHAN I JUST DON'T FEEL
LIKE MYSELF SINCE THAT
BIG METEOR SHOWER.**

KnOcK, kNoCk.

Who's there?

RON.

Ron who?

RON A LITTLE FASTER BECAUSE I SEE A RAPTOR OVER THERE!

KnOcK, kNoCk.

Who's there?

STAMP.

Stamp who?

STAMPEDE! LOOK OUT!

KnOcK, kNoCk.

Who's there?

DOZEN.

Dozen who?

DOZEN ANYBODY HERE KNOW HOW TO SPELL PTERANODON?

KnOcK, kNoCk.

Who's there?

CARNOTAUR.

Carnotaur who?

CARNO-TAURED FROM WALKING ALL THIS WAY, AREN'T YOU?

KnOcK, kNoCk.

Who's there?

CARNOTAUR.

Carnotaur who?

CRUNCH!

KnOcK, kNoCk.

Who's there?

HERB.

Herb who?

**HERB IVORE.
GOT ANY VEGETABLES?**

KnOcK, kNoCk.

Who's there?

SURI.

Suri who?

SURI WE CAN'T GO ON LIKE THIS!

KnOcK, kNoCk.

Who's there?

EEMA.

Eema who?

EEMA GETTIN' TIRED OF KNOCK-KNOCKS, AREN'T YOU?

KnOcK, kNoCk.

Who's there?

NORMA LEE.

Norma Lee who?

**NORMA LEE WE DON'T
HAVE TO MIGRATE THIS
FAR, BUT THE WATER HOLES
HAVE DRIED UP!**

KnOcK, kNoCk.

Who's there?

JUICY.

Juicy who?

**JUICY THAT REALLY
BIG BRACHIOSAUR?**

KnOcK, kNoCk.

Who's there?

CHARLOTTE.

Charlotte who?

CHARLOTTE OF DINOSAURS IN THE HERD.

KnOcK, kNoCk.

Who's there?

THE.

The who?

THE END OF ALL THESE SILLY DINOSAUR JOKES.

THE BEHIND-THE-SCENES SCOOP ON THE MAKING OF THE DINOSAUR MOVIE

Disney's **DINOSAUR** used real-life backgrounds filmed in Hawaii, Venezuela, Jordan, Samoa, Australia and the deserts of California.

The Ritual Tree is actually a model that stands over fifty feet tall! Animators wrapped digital textures around the model to make it look lifelike. Every leaf is also animated by digital artists.

Animators spent hours
riding on the backs of elephants
to figure out how they could
make Baylene walk.

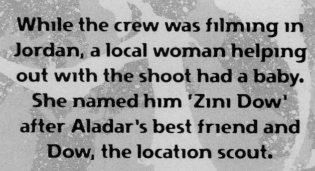

While the crew was filming in
Jordan, a local woman helping
out with the shoot had a baby.
She named him 'Zini Dow'
after Aladar's best friend and
Dow, the location scout.

No one knows what colours
real dinosaurs were. Colours
were assigned based on each
character's personality.

The carnotaurs are red because
they're dangerous and angry.

Aladar is a cool blue-green
because he's so cool-headed.

The big lake that Zini surfs in
is not a real lake! All of the water
was created by digital artists.

When Aladar jumps off the
cliff to escape the Fireball, there
are bits of meteor flying all
around the sky. The pieces of the
Fireball were actually created
by a spark machine placed
over a pool at a water park
in California!

The cliff Aladar jumps off
of is a real cliff in Hawaii.
The ocean below is the pool
at a Californian water park!

The sound team on this film
used a variety of animal sounds
to create all of the ancient
calls and roars. For example:

raptor growl =
the altered sound
of a chihuahua with asthma!

lemur calls =
the blending of a penguin
call and a fox howl.

Animators used fossilized
dinosaur skin as inspiration
to create the complex patterns
and textures on Aladar and
other iguanodons.